POCKET
prayers
for TEACHERS

POCKET prayers

for TEACHERS

40 SIMPLE PRAYERS THAT BRING PEACE AND RENEWAL

MAX LUCADO

WITH JENNIFER K. HALE

THOMAS NELSON
Since 1798

Published in Nashville, Tennessee, by Thomas Nelson. Thomas Nelson is a registered trademark of HarperCollins Christian Publishing, Inc.

Thomas Nelson titles may be purchased in bulk for educational, business, fund-raising, or sales promotional use. For information, please e-mail SpecialMarkets@ThomasNelson.com.

Unless otherwise noted, Scripture quotations are taken from the New King James Version®. © 1982 by Thomas Nelson. Used by permission. All rights reserved.

Scripture quotations marked NCV are from the New Century Version®. © 2005 by Thomas Nelson. Used by permission. All rights reserved.

Scripture quotations marked NIV are from the Holy Bible, New International Version®, NIV®. Copyright © 1973, 1978, 1984, 2011 by Biblica, Inc.® Used by permission of Zondervan. All rights reserved worldwide. www.zondervan.com. The "NIV" and "New International Version" are trademarks registered in the United States Patent and Trademark Office by Biblica, Inc.®

Scripture quotations marked NLT are from the *Holy Bible*, New Living Translation. © 1996, 2004, 2007, 2013 by Tyndale House Foundation. Used by permission of Tyndale House Publishers, Inc., Carol Stream, Illinois 60188. All rights reserved.

Any Internet addresses, phone numbers, or company or product information printed in this book are offered as a resource and are not intended in any way to be or to imply an endorsement by Thomas Nelson, nor does Thomas Nelson vouch for the existence, content, or services of these sites, phone numbers, companies, or products beyond the life of this book.

ISBN 978-0-7180-7836-5 (eBook)

Library of Congress Control Number: 2015956803
ISBN 978-0-7180-7736-5

Printed in Mexico

16 17 18 19 20   RRD   10 9 8 7 6 5 4 3 2 1

The Pocket Prayer

Hello, my name is Max. I'm a recovering prayer wimp. I doze off when I pray. My thoughts zig, then zag, then zig again. Distractions swarm like gnats on a summer night. If attention deficit disorder applies to prayer, I am afflicted. When I pray, I think of a thousand things I need to do. I forget the one thing I set out to do: pray.

Some people excel in prayer. They inhale heaven and exhale God. They are the SEAL Team Six of intercession. They would rather pray than sleep. Why is it that I sleep when I pray? They belong to the PGA: Prayer Giants Association. I am a card-carrying member of the PWA: Prayer Wimps Anonymous.

Can you relate? It's not that we don't pray at all. We all pray some.

On tearstained pillows we pray.

In grand liturgies we pray.

At the sight of geese in flight, we pray.

Quoting ancient devotions, we pray.

We pray to stay sober, centered, or solvent. We pray when the lump is deemed malignant. When the money runs out before the month does. When the unborn baby hasn't kicked in a while. We all pray . . . some.

But wouldn't we all like to pray . . .

More?

Better?

Deeper?

Stronger?

With more fire, faith, or fervency?

Yet we have kids to feed, bills to pay, deadlines to meet.

The calendar pounces on our good intentions like a tiger on a rabbit. We want to pray, but *when*?

We want to pray, but *why*? We might as well admit it. Prayer is odd, peculiar. Speaking into space. Lifting words into the sky. We can't even get the cable company to answer us, yet God will? The doctor is too busy, but God isn't? We have our doubts about prayer.

And we have our checkered history with prayer: unmet expectations, unanswered requests. We can barely genuflect for the scar tissue on our knees. God, to some, is the ultimate heartbreaker. Why keep tossing the coins of our longings into a silent pool? He jilted me once . . . but not twice.

Oh, the peculiar puzzle of prayer.

We aren't the first to struggle. The sign-up sheet for Prayer 101 contains some familiar names: the apostles John, James, Andrew, and Peter. When one of Jesus' disciples requested, "Lord, teach us to pray" (Luke 11:1 NIV), none of the others objected. No one walked away saying, "Hey, I have prayer figured out." The first followers of Jesus needed prayer guidance.

In fact, the only tutorial they ever requested was on prayer.

The first followers of Jesus needed prayer guidance.

They could have asked for instructions on many topics: bread multiplying, speech making, storm stilling. Jesus raised people from the dead. But a "How to Vacate the Cemetery" seminar? His followers never called for one. But they did want him to do this: "Lord, teach us to pray."

Might their interest have had something to do with the jaw-dropping, eye-popping promises Jesus attached to prayer? "Ask and it will be given to you" (Matt. 7:7 NIV). "If you believe, you will get anything you ask for in prayer" (Matt. 21:22 NCV). Jesus never attached such power to other endeavors. "*Plan* and it will be given to you." "You will get anything you *work* for." Those words are not in the Bible. But these are—"If you remain in me and follow my teachings, you can ask anything you want, and it will be given to you" (John 15:7 NCV).

Jesus gave stunning prayer promises.

And he set a compelling prayer example. Jesus prayed before he ate. He prayed for children. He prayed for the sick. He prayed with thanks. He prayed with tears. He had made the planets and shaped the stars, yet he prayed. He is the Lord of angels and Commander of heavenly hosts, yet he prayed. He is coequal with God, the exact representation of the Holy One, and yet he devoted himself to prayer. He prayed in the desert, cemetery, and garden. "He went out and departed to a solitary place; and there He prayed" (Mark 1:35).

This dialogue must have been common among his friends:

"Has anyone seen Jesus?"

"Oh, you know. He's up to the same thing."

"Praying *again*?"

"Yep. He's been gone since sunrise."

Jesus would even disappear for an entire night of prayer. I'm thinking of one occasion in particular. He'd just experienced one of the most stressful days of his ministry. The day began with the news of the death of his relative John the Baptist. Jesus sought to retreat with his disciples, yet a throng of thousands followed him. Though grief-stricken, he spent the day teaching and healing people. When it was discovered that the host of people had no food to eat, Jesus multiplied bread out of a basket and fed the entire multitude. In the span of a few hours, he battled sorrow, stress, demands, and needs. He deserved a good night's rest. Yet when evening finally came, he told the crowd to leave and the disciples to board their boat, and "he went up into the hills by himself to pray" (Mark 6:46 NLT).

Apparently it was the correct choice. A storm exploded over the Sea of Galilee, leaving the disciples "in trouble far away from land, for a strong wind had risen, and they were fighting heavy waves. About three o'clock in the morning Jesus came toward them, walking on the water" (Matt. 14:24–25 NLT). Jesus ascended the mountain depleted. He reappeared invigorated. When he reached the water, he never broke his stride. You'd have thought the water was a park lawn and the storm a spring breeze.

Do you think the disciples made the prayer–power connection? "Lord, teach us to pray *like that*. Teach us to find strength in prayer. To banish fear in prayer. To defy storms in prayer. To come off the mountain of prayer with the authority of a prince."

What about you? The disciples faced angry waves and a watery grave. You face angry clients, a turbulent economy, raging seas of stress and sorrow.

"Lord," we still request, "teach us to pray."

When the disciples asked Jesus to teach them to pray, he gave them a prayer. Not a lecture on prayer. Not the doctrine of prayer. He gave them a quotable, repeatable, portable prayer (Luke 11:1–4).

Could you use the same? It seems to me that the prayers of the Bible can be distilled into one. The result is a simple, easy-to-remember, pocket-size prayer:

Father,
> *you are good.*
>> *I need help. Heal me and forgive me.*
>> *They need help.*
>> *Thank you.*
>> *In Jesus' name, amen.*

Let this prayer punctuate your day. As you begin your morning, *Father, you are good.* As you commute to work or walk the hallways at school, *I need help.* As you wait in the grocery line, *They need help.* Keep this prayer in your pocket as you pass through the day.

When we invite God into our world, he walks in. He brings

a host of gifts: joy, patience, resilience. Anxieties come, but they don't stick. Fears surface and then depart. Regrets land on the windshield, but then comes the wiper of prayer. The devil still hands me stones of guilt, but I turn and give them to Christ. I'm completing my sixth decade, yet I'm wired with energy. I am happier, healthier, and more hopeful than I have ever been. Struggles come, for sure. But so does God.

Prayer is not a privilege for the pious, not the art of a chosen few. Prayer is simply a heartfelt conversation between God and his child.

Prayer is not a privilege for the pious, not the art of a chosen few. Prayer is simply a heartfelt conversation between God and his child. My friend, he wants to talk with you. Even now, as you read these words, he taps at the door. Open it. Welcome him in. Let the conversation begin.

Prayers for Inspiration and Encouragement

1

---

*Speak to each other with psalms, hymns,
and spiritual songs, singing and making
music in your hearts to the Lord. Always
give thanks to God the Father for everything,
in the name of our Lord Jesus Christ.*

EPHESIANS 5:19-20 NCV

Heavenly Father, you are the great provider, and you always take care of me. You give me reason to sing.

When I have good days, let me have a thankful heart. When my days are long and I'm tired, give me a thankful heart then too. Whether things are easy and I love my job or teaching is harder than ever and I'm questioning everything, remind me to praise you.

Also remind my coworkers what a privilege it is to be a teacher. Give them thankful hearts for the school, the leadership, their jobs, and their students.

Thank you for my job, Lord. Even on the most difficult days, I'm grateful to have it.

In your Son's precious name, amen.

2

You formed my inward parts; You covered me in my mother's womb. I will praise You, for I am fearfully and wonderfully made; marvelous are Your works, and that my soul knows very well.

PSALM 139:13-14

Holy God, what you create is beautiful. You never make a mistake; everything you do is perfect.

Each student in my class is precious. Each one is a gift, and you created them exactly the way you wanted them to be. Help me see the beauty in your creation. Don't let me take any of them for granted.

Help the teachers and administrators in my school see your fingerprints on every student. Let each challenge be seen as an opportunity for good; let each character trait be seen as a reflection of your glory.

As I think of all my students by name, I thank you for creating them and for what you will do through them in the future.

In your name, amen.

3

---

*Let the beauty of the L*ORD *our God be upon us, and establish the work of our hands for us; yes, establish the work of our hands.*

PSALM 90:17

Everlasting Father, your works are wonderful, and your glory is limitless.

In everything I do—at home, at school, in the community—bless my work. Only you can see inside my heart and know that I want to do a good job and be a witness for you. Give me the ability to teach and to love and to take advantage of each opportunity you send me. Remind me that others are counting on me to work hard and do well.

Help the principals, teachers, counselors, and other staff see the importance of their jobs as they go into schools every day. Give them a daily dose of joy and excitement for their tasks.

Thank you for entrusting me with the pleasure and responsibility of guiding minds and hearts.

In your Son's precious name, amen.

4

Through the LORD's mercies we are not consumed, because His compassions fail not. They are new every morning; great is Your faithfulness. "The LORD is my portion," says my soul, "therefore I hope in Him!"

LAMENTATIONS 3:22-24

You are the great I AM—eternal and unchanging—yet your mercy is always fresh and new. Magnificent is your holy name!

Whether it's the dawning of a new school year, a new semester, or a new day, give me excitement about the opportunity in each new situation. Remind me that being a teacher means I have the chance every day to change a life. Push me to take that chance.

Prompt my students to take advantage of new opportunities as they grow into adults. Help them discern good decision making and find delight in each day.

Thank you for new mercies. Thank you for school years filled with joy and the chance to do something great.

In your name, amen.

5

___

Whether you turn to the right or to the left,
your ears will hear a voice behind you,
saying, "This is the way; walk in it."

ISAIAH 30:21 NIV

Mighty God, you are omniscient. You know all, see all, and understand all things. You created everything in your time and for your purpose.

Sometimes I feel as though I have no idea what I'm doing. There are days I worry that I'm failing my students, that maybe I've even chosen the wrong career. Would you remind me I'm not alone? Let me hear your voice and your words of soothing reassurance.

When my teacher friends are confused and feel lost, please whisper hints of your love, reassuring them that, no matter what, you are always present and you are in control.

Thank you for being the Lord of my life. Thank you for guiding me each moment and for demonstrating your eternal love.

In Christ's name, amen.

6

---

*The LORD your God is with you, the Mighty
Warrior who saves. He will take great delight
in you; in his love he will no longer rebuke
you, but will rejoice over you with singing.*

ZEPHANIAH 3:17 NIV

Holy Father, your love is endless. You know everything about me—the pleasures and burdens of my heart—and you sing songs of joy over me.

Some days are perfect. My students respond well to my lessons, and I am reminded why I chose to be a teacher. Prompt me to thank you and to share my joy with those around me.

Bless my colleagues with good days. Remind them of the pleasure of teaching, and give them reasons to have happiness in their hearts. Let them delight in every child in their charge.

Thank you for the good days. Thank you for making joy contagious.

In your glorious name, amen.

7

He will yet fill your mouth with laughter
and your lips with shouts of joy.

JOB 8:21 NIV

L ord, you reign over all things and delight in your creation. You have given me a gift in each student I work with. Their joy is infectious and their laughter contagious. Their humor is often just what I need to get through a tough day, and I praise you for that.

Help my coworkers find enjoyment in what they do. Let the laughter of children resonate in their hearts.

Thank you for laughter and its healing properties. Thank you for the memories made with my students every day.

In the name of Jesus, amen.

8

Be strong and take heart, all
*you who hope in the L*ORD*.*

PSALM 31:24 NIV

Precious Lord, you are faithful and true, and you never change.

It feels as if the world of education changes all the time—new ideas, new laws, new requirements. In a shifting world remind me that my hope is in you. I don't want to misplace my faith by putting it in man-made standards. I want my faith firmly grounded in your standards, your promises, and your truth.

When my colleagues are caught up in the swirl of change, remind them to be strong and faithful. When the students are overtested and underachieving, help us show them their true worth as children of God.

Thank you for never changing and for always keeping your promises. I know you have the world in your hands.

In Jesus' name, amen.

9

At that time the disciples came to Jesus, saying, "Who then is greatest in the kingdom of heaven?" Then Jesus called a little child to Him, set him in the midst of them, and said, "Assuredly, I say to you, unless you are converted and become as little children, you will by no means enter the kingdom of heaven."

MATTHEW 18:1-3

Father God, you have created so many gifts in this world. Praise your precious name!

Daily give me wisdom to know how to love the young children in my class, even in the tough moments. Give me patience to deal with unexpected classroom situations. Fill my heart with sweet memories of every child.

Bless each student in my class, especially those from troubled homes. Let them feel my love and attention, and please protect their innocence. Show me how to be their steady, dependable guide.

Thank you for the sweetness and goodness of children. Thank you for calling me to the task of teaching these little ones and for honoring me with this precious responsibility.

In Jesus' name, amen.

Prayers for Clarity
and Creativity

10

If any of you lacks wisdom, let him ask of God, who gives to all liberally and without reproach, and it will be given to him.

JAMES 1:5

God, you are Jehovah-jireh, the giver of everything. You take care of me even before I can ask for help.

You gave me the talent to teach. When I am feeling uninspired and need new ideas, reignite the passion in me. Give me wisdom, and help me use my imagination to create new ways to reach my students. Let me be an effective teacher by using my gifts from you.

Help my coteachers tap into their talents and use them well. Let your glory shine in their skills so we can celebrate the achievement of our students through your mighty work.

Thank you for the talents you've so generously poured on my colleagues and me. Thank you for abilities that make us diverse and beautiful in your eyes.

In Jesus' name, amen.

11

Add to your faith virtue, to virtue knowledge, to knowledge self-control, to self-control perseverance, to perseverance godliness, to godliness brotherly kindness, and to brotherly kindness love. For if these things are yours and abound, you will be neither barren nor unfruitful.

2 Peter 1:5-8

Mighty God, you are good. You give strength, knowledge, wisdom, and mercy in abundance, and my cup runs over.

I want to be an effective teacher. I want to pass on not only knowledge but also your love to my students, letting them see you even if I can't always use your name. Let me be productive in my work. Help my students excel in their curriculum and also learn character in my classroom.

Bless our school. Unify our faculty; give us common goals. Help us get along and love one another so we can work together well to serve our students.

Thank you for loving and giving. Thank you for pouring yourself into my life. Your mercy is my strength.

In your name, amen.

12

The fear of the LORD is the instruction of wisdom, and before honor is humility.

PROVERBS 15:33

My God in heaven, I praise you, for you alone are worthy of praise.

Sometimes I get too caught up in the details of my life. Help me remember that I have no idea what goes on in the homes of my students. Give me ears to listen and eyes to see. Let me learn from them, and remind me that their life experiences, although different from mine, are valuable.

Protect my students, Lord. When they leave me, go with them. Open their hearts to what I'm trying to teach them so we can learn from each other. Help them learn more than facts, help them learn values and the beginnings of wisdom.

Thank you for all the students in my class and their families.

In Christ's name, amen.

13

---

*There is a time for everything, and a season for
every activity under the heavens: . . . a time to
plant and a time to uproot, a time to kill and
a time to heal, a time to tear down and a time
to build, a time to weep and a time to laugh.*

ECCLESIASTES 3:1-4 NIV

God, you are the ultimate timekeeper. You have mapped the perfect plan for our lives and know the number of our days.

Help me discern good timing—to know the time for firm discipline in my classroom and the time for laughter, to recognize when students need a listening ear and open arms and when they need advice and counsel.

Help my students know the importance of an education. Give them goals that will motivate them, and give them the means to achieve those goals.

Thank you for your plans, for they are greater than ours.

In your eternal name, amen.

14

---

*Instruct the wise and they will be
wiser still; teach the righteous and
they will add to their learning.*

PROVERBS 9:9 NIV

Father in heaven, you are the source of all knowledge, the provider of all things great and small.

Please give me a mentor—someone who can provide ideas and techniques that will make me a better teacher. Remind me that I became a teacher because I love to learn. Give me a heart willing to listen and the ability to mentor someone else in the future.

As teachers near retirement, bless their work. Instill in them the desire to mentor newer teachers and to pass on their strategies and plans, helping newer teachers impact lives for coming generations.

Thank you for the wisdom of talented teachers. Thank you for making me a lifelong student.

In Christ's name, amen.

15

Whoever gives heed to instruction prospers,
*and blessed is the one who trusts in the L*ORD.

PROVERBS 16:20 NIV

Jesus, your teaching instructs my heart and soul. There is no one greater than you.

Make me eager to listen to and learn from others. Sometimes professional development seems unnecessary, but give me a willing heart to learn and to apply new ideas to my classroom so I can grow as a teacher.

Give the administrators the ability to see when teachers need more encouragement and help in order to make our schools and students stronger.

Thank you for being the example of the ultimate teacher. Thank you for mercy and grace and for showing us the value of living each day by walking in the ways you've laid out for us.

In your holy name, amen.

16

God is able to bless you abundantly, so that in all things at all times, having all that you need, you will abound in every good work.

2 Corinthians 9:8 niv

God, through your gifts you pour your unending love over us. You bless us so we can bless others.

Please give me clarity of mind and an extra dose of creativity when I'm working on lesson plans. Help me develop the skills to differentiate learning styles and to engage my students through varied activities.

Give my students the ability to comprehend the lessons, to grow, and to enjoy their school days. Even when the classes aren't fun, help them appreciate the challenge of mastering new skills.

Thank you for blessing me. Thank you for your goodness and your mercy. And thank you for each day and each lesson that allows me to call myself a teacher.

In your name, amen.

17

Let my teaching fall like rain and my words
descend like dew, like showers on new grass,
like abundant rain on tender plants.

DEUTERONOMY 32:2 NIV

Father, your words are the foundation of my heart's belief. You are the rock on which I depend.

Help me engage my students each day by capturing their attention, piquing their curiosity, fueling their desire to learn, and encouraging them to participate in class. Let my words water their thirsty minds and my love grow relationships with them and among them.

Give my coworkers a passion for engagement and the drive to use the personalities you created in them to reach each student. Help them use words of encouragement to foster student growth.

Thank you that the Holy Spirit engages me through your Word and that your promises cover me like soft rain.

In Jesus' name, amen.

Prayers for Love
and Patience

18

---

*He will give the rain for your seed with which
you sow the ground, and bread of the increase
of the earth; it will be fat and plentiful.*

ISAIAH 30:23

Loving Father, your harvest is bountiful. You give me the delight of seeing my students grow and change daily. Only you deserve glory and honor and praise.

Rain down your mercy upon me, so my legacy will be quality teaching sprinkled with kindness, compassion, and a sense of humor. Let my classroom be remembered as a joyous, safe place.

Please help my students feel your loving presence in all areas of their lives. When they feel out of place or alone, remind them that you are ever present. Grow them into loving adults who bless others in your name.

Thank you for loving us enough to nurture us through your Word.

In your name, amen.

19

But the fruit of the Spirit is love, joy,
peace, longsuffering, kindness, goodness,
faithfulness, gentleness, self-control.
Against such there is no law.

GALATIANS 5:22–23

Heavenly Father, you are the source of joy, peace, and love, which is shown through your Son's sacrifice on the cross.

On the days when my patience is thin, when my students are acting up and I fear I'll express my frustration, remind me of your mercy toward me. Take away the frazzled feelings of stress, and replace them with heaping portions of self-control seasoned with patience and flavored with kindness.

When my coworkers are at the end of their ropes, help them hold on. Calm their spirits, and remind them that you see each precious child, each stressful situation, each moment of frustration.

Thank you for setting an example for us through your Son, who lived out the fruit of the Spirit in every way. Thank you for making me more like him every day.

In his precious name, amen.

20

Bear with each other and forgive one another
if any of you has a grievance against
someone. Forgive as the Lord forgave you.
And over all these virtues put on love, which
binds them all together in perfect unity.

COLOSSIANS 3:13-14 NIV

Father, your forgiveness stretches as far as the east is from the west. You humble me with your love.

When I'm hurt, it's sometimes difficult for me to let it go. If a student is wild and disobedient or a colleague is critical of me, I want to hold a grudge. Soften my heart with whispered reminders of your grace and forgiveness. Remind me that the point is not whether someone else deserves mercy, because I'm a sinner in need of mercy too.

God, help us love one another. Help my students get along and form lasting friendships. Bless the friendships I have with my coworkers, and guide us to work through problems with compassion and understanding.

Thank you for making the ultimate sacrifice for unworthy human hearts. Thank you for loving your creation that much.

In Jesus' name, amen.

21

___

Beloved, if God so loved us, we also ought to love one another. No one has seen God at any time. If we love one another, God abides in us, and His love has been perfected in us.

1 John 4:11-12

God, your love covers all sin, and it washes us white as snow.

Help me love the student who seems unlovable. She's disruptive and rude, and some days I want to pretend she's not there. Soften my heart so I can see her through your eyes and understand why she acts out and how I can reach her. Give me wisdom and compassion.

Father, touch this student's heart. If she learns nothing else in my classroom, teach her through my actions that you are a mighty God, who loves her unconditionally. Let me be your example.

Thank you for loving me when I'm unlovable. Thank you for forgiving me and for seeing my soul and finding it worthy of salvation.

In your Son's name, amen.

22

The things which you learned and received
and heard and saw in me, these do, and
the God of peace will be with you.

PHILIPPIANS 4:9

G od, all glory and honor be to you, who gave us Jesus, our Savior!

As I learn from your Word, let me put that wisdom into practice in my life. Help me improve classroom management by having high expectations for myself and modeling them for my students. I want to handle my students with loving discipline, as you often handle me.

I pray that my teacher friends will improve their classroom management by learning new techniques and growing closer to you as they apply your Word to their lives.

Thank you for loving me enough to guide my footsteps. Thank you for reminding me that applying your truths helps me grow in your love.

In your holy name, amen.

23

Though one may be overpowered by another, two can withstand him. And a threefold cord is not quickly broken.

Ecclesiastes 4:12

Father in heaven, you are the fountain of truth, and you make constant declarations of your love.

Remind me that when I have a good idea or a successful classroom strategy, I can support other teachers by sharing it. Help me do that in a spirit of love, offering aid and collaboration without appearing as if I think I'm superior.

Let my colleagues be open to sharing with me, and let us all receive help with the goal of student success in mind. Humble us, open our hearts, and keep us grounded in the spirit of being a family within our school.

Thank you for your love. Thank you for teaching us how to give and receive and for making us better through collaboration.

In your name, amen.

Prayers for Peace
and Protection

24

We may boldly say: "The LORD is my helper;
I will not fear. What can man do to me?"

HEBREWS 13:6

Almighty God, you are powerful. You possess all authority over heaven and earth.

This world can be a scary place. Even our schools don't seem safe from those who do evil. God, protect my school. Put your shield over it, and in frightening moments, blanket everyone within its walls with peace. Replace fear with the power of your love.

Protect my students from those who would hurt them. Protect my friends and coworkers, and prompt them to look to you for peace in times of trouble.

Thank you for being the God who loves us enough to protect our souls for all eternity through your Son, Jesus.

In his glorious name, amen.

25

Let the peace of God rule in your
hearts, to which also you were called
in one body; and be thankful.

COLOSSIANS 3:15

Father, you are the God of peace that surpasses all understanding.

Since I work closely with so many people, conflicts are bound to arise. When they do, remind me of your ways. Remind me of the importance of being a peacemaker because I am part of the body of Christ. Keep me from the sin of arguing, and instead help me focus on loving those around me.

God, bless my classroom with peace, and help me teach my students to speak words of kindness to one another. In the hallways remind me to speak words of encouragement to my coworkers and words of respect to our administration.

Thank you for the joy of human relationships. Thank you for sending the Prince of Peace for us all.

In his name, amen.

26

Peace I leave with you, My peace I give to you;
not as the world gives do I give to you. Let not
your heart be troubled, neither let it be afraid.

Heavenly Father, you are the creator of this world and all its beauty. You are the God who sees me and the One who made me just for this time and place.

When I am stressed because of situations with students, decisions made by the administration, or even the amount of work teaching requires, give me your peace. Replace the shallow reassurances of the world with your holy presence so my heart will be calm.

Bring peace to my colleagues too. Stifle stress with your joy. Give us a positive outlook on the future of education, and keep us from being pessimistic.

In a world where daily life is often measured by stress level, thank you for providing the calm that is beyond all understanding.

In your majestic name, amen.

27

---

*These things I have spoken to you, that
in Me you may have peace. In the world
you will have tribulation; but be of good
cheer, I have overcome the world.*

JOHN 16:33

God, you are our rock and our salvation. In you we trust completely, for you are the mighty conqueror who has overcome the world!

When tragedy strikes, whether it affects our homes, the families of our students, our friends, or our school community, protect us from anger and retaliation. You have loved us enough to overcome sin and conquer death.

When the people around us struggle to understand, provide peace, comfort, and the blessing of your grace.

Thank you for wrapping your loving arms around us. Thank you for being our rock and for providing eternal life so that someday all sadness and evil will end.

In your Son's perfect name, amen.

28

Blessed is the man who walks not in the
counsel of the ungodly, nor stands in the path
of sinners, nor sits in the seat of the scornful;
but his delight is in the law of the LORD, and
in His law he meditates day and night.

PSALM 1:1-2

Father, you are the mighty lawgiver, and you alone are worthy of worship!

Help me protect my students. Give me the courage to fight for what is right on their behalf and to be an example of truth. Teach me your law so well that I can recognize when I need to defend the defenseless.

Protect our young students, Lord. They are exposed to so much ugliness early in their lives. Shield their minds, keep their thoughts clean, and help them choose good over evil. Give them wisdom, and meet their basic needs so they can focus on learning.

Thank you for providing your law so we can always know right from wrong.

In your powerful name, amen.

29

You shall not hate your brother in your heart.
You shall surely rebuke your neighbor, and
not bear sin because of him. You shall not take
vengeance, nor bear any grudge against the
children of your people, but you shall love
your neighbor as yourself: I am the LORD.

LEVITICUS 19:17-18

Lord, you are the salvation of the world. You are the source of light and love for this world. Holy are you!

When I have to deal with difficult parents or guardians of my students, give me words that will bring peace to the conversation. Help me communicate directly and with a grace that glorifies you. Calm my emotions and keep me far from anger.

Bless the parents, Lord. Give them a willingness to listen and to respect my expertise as an educator. Most of all, bless the relationship between the parents and their children—the students in my class.

Thank you for your command to love. It reminds me that I'm to treat everyone with grace, just as you treat me.

In your precious name, amen.

Prayers for
Integrity and Grace

30

In the multitude of words sin is not lacking,
but he who restrains his lips is wise.

PROVERBS 10:19

Heavenly Father, you are holy. You are untainted and perfect.

Sometimes I talk too much and say things I later regret. Sometimes, I confess, I listen to gossip when I should walk away. When I am tempted to say more than I should, including hurtful chatter, prompt me to keep quiet. Help me speak only words of compassion and love, words that uplift and glorify you.

When gossip threatens the relationships of my coworkers, erase it with kindness and close every mouth. Help those in my school to focus on the work, building up rather than tearing down one another. Keep our words few, and multiply our accomplishments.

Thank you for language so we can express our joy and love for you.

In your name, amen.

31

---

*All Scripture is given by inspiration of God,
and is profitable for doctrine, for reproof, for
correction, for instruction in righteousness,
that the man of God may be complete,
thoroughly equipped for every good work.*

2 TIMOTHY 3:16-17

Gracious heavenly Father, you breathed life into the world. Your presence surrounds me, and your Word stands forever.

When I'm challenged by my students, help me remember that the truth of your Word is the guideline I should use for correction and discipline.

I pray that my students will absorb something of you in my classroom so they will be better equipped for the world. Help them grow stronger and wiser in the time they are with me.

Thank you for your unchanging Word. Thank you that I can use it as my guideline for daily living. Knowing that my faith and life are grounded in your truth gives me the strength I need for such a responsibility as teaching and molding young minds.

In your glorious and holy name, amen.

32

"The eyes of the LORD are on the righteous, and His ears are open to their prayers; but the face of the LORD is against those who do evil." And who is he who will harm you if you become followers of what is good? But even if you should suffer for righteousness' sake, you are blessed.

1 PETER 3:12-14

Father in heaven, you are the ultimate judge of righteousness. Your ways are holy and fair.

I work hard, Lord, and sometimes I don't feel that I get any recognition. Sometimes I'm criticized for making the right choices in a world that no longer values honesty. When these things happen, remind me that your love and recognition are more valuable than any earthly acknowledgments.

When my colleagues would rather be popular than do what is right, convict their hearts. Bring them back to your truth.

Thank you for your mercy when we fail, Lord. Thank you for your strength and love when we feel persecuted. Most of all, thank you for letting us work for your kingdom.

In your blessed name, amen.

33

---

*In all things showing yourself to be a
pattern of good works; in doctrine showing
integrity, reverence, incorruptibility, sound
speech that cannot be condemned, that
one who is an opponent may be ashamed,
having nothing evil to say of you.*

TITUS 2:7-8

Lord, your holiness is untainted. We cannot fathom the beauty of your greatness.

I'm never going to be perfect, God, but I want to be an example of your kingdom in every moment of my life. In situations where I can't expressly say your name, let my actions speak louder than words ever could.

I pray that the Holy Spirit will prompt the hearts of the students and teachers around me to want to know you more. Help them recognize that "something different" in me—your peace and your presence.

Thank you for saving my soul so I might be your witness. Thank you for each precious student in my class. I know you put every one of them there for a reason.

In Christ's name, amen.

34

Whoever desires to become great among you, let him be your servant. And whoever desires to be first among you, let him be your slave—just as the Son of Man did not come to be served, but to serve, and to give His life a ransom for many.

MATTHEW 20:26-28

Jesus, you saved us from our sins even though we didn't deserve your sacrifice. Glorious is your name!

I'm in a position of leadership within the school, and I ask you to remind me of your example. You were the greatest leader of all mankind, yet you came to serve. Let me be a servant to those I'm leading so their jobs may be even more rewarding.

Help those in my school extend support to the leadership even when they don't understand difficult decisions that are made. Prompt them to agree with the common cause—our students.

Thank you for those with whom I work. Thank you for those I lead. Help me follow your example as I serve them.

In your name, amen.

Prayers for Strength and Endurance

35

My dear brothers and sisters, stand firm. Let nothing move you. Always give yourselves fully to the work of the Lord, because you know that your labor in the Lord is not in vain.

1 CORINTHIANS 15:58 NIV

Heavenly Father, your eternal love knows no measure. You and your love are beyond what our minds can even imagine.

Sometimes I feel very discouraged when I spend hours planning and don't get the results I want. I hear a voice that calls me inadequate. Remind me that I'm more than adequate because of your love.

Help my colleagues understand your Word. Remind them that what they do is about so much more than numbers, data, and standardized test scores. Remind them that the hearts they touch are much more important than any measurable result.

Thank you for giving me the opportunity to touch the heart of a child today. It's a gift I don't take for granted.

In Christ's holy name, amen.

36

The word of God is alive and active.
Sharper than any double-edged sword,
it penetrates even to dividing soul and
spirit, joints and marrow; it judges the
thoughts and attitudes of the heart.

HEBREWS 4:12 NIV

My God, you are alive and always active. Not a single moment escapes you. Not one thought or deed goes unnoticed.

I often depend on my routine to get through the day. I need that cup of coffee, that soda, or that chocolate. But remind me that your Word is more powerful than any jolt of caffeine. Let your truth flow through me, giving me energy to get through each day. Let your power infuse me!

When those around me need your strength, bless them with energy that is beyond anything humans can create. Let them walk and run and not grow weary or faint.

Thank you for being all that I need.

In your name, amen.

37

Brothers and sisters, we instructed you how to live in order to please God, as in fact you are living. Now we ask you and urge you in the Lord Jesus to do this more and more.

1 THESSALONIANS 4:1 NIV

Father in heaven, you are the giver of truth. You instruct me through your Word, and I want to keep learning.

Sometimes I feel unmotivated. I'm burned out from the daily grind and endless requirements. Remind me that life isn't about pleasing others but pleasing you. Give me fuel through your Word, and inspire me to live each moment for you.

When my coworkers need motivation, let me be a cheerleader. When I need motivation, let them bring words of encouragement, so together we can create a positive school culture that's contagious.

Thank you for educators who work hard. Thank you for your example through Jesus Christ.

In his holy name, amen.

38

Never be lacking in zeal, but keep your
spiritual fervor, serving the Lord.

ROMANS 12:11 NIV

Heavenly Father, your love is our banner and triumph. We rejoice in you!

You instilled a passion in me—a passion for students, for teaching, and for learning. God, keep the flames of that passion burning brightly. Remind me often that teaching is much more than the requirements of my state and school. It's about loving, encouraging, and sparking a passion for learning in my students.

Let something in my classroom pique their interest. Help them discover a talent or an interest that drives their desire to learn and to seek a future as bright as your love and light.

Thank you for making me a teacher. I love what I do, and I love you, Lord.

In Christ's name, amen.

39

_____

If you faithfully obey the commands I am giving you today—to love the LORD your God and to serve him with all your heart and with all your soul—then I will send rain on your land in its season. . . . I will provide grass in the fields for your cattle, and you will eat and be satisfied.

DEUTERONOMY 11:13-15 NIV

Most High God, you are unchanging. You are present in every moment of eternity.

On the days I am weary and weak, give me strength. Remind me that as long as I put you first in my life, you will give me the wisdom and encouragement I need to do my job as a teacher and to see it as a gift.

God, remind my colleagues of your promises. Instill in them a hunger to do their jobs well. Lead those who have lost their passion for teaching to their true calling so they may be blessed as you planned.

Thank you for revealing my calling through each and every student I've known.

In your name, amen.

40

Then the apostles gathered to Jesus and told Him all things, both what they had done and what they had taught. And He said to them, "Come aside by yourselves to a deserted place and rest a while." For there were many coming and going, and they did not even have time to eat.

MARK 6:30-31

God, you are the giver of peace, the restorer of my soul. When I am exhausted, give me rest. Help me know when I need to slow down and when I need to set aside time to recharge. If I'm tempted to take on too much, help me find the balance in life, and remind me that my relationship with you and my family must be priorities.

Give breaks to tired educators. Restore energy to their bodies, inspiration to their minds, and excitement to their souls. Protect them from the fatigue of overworking.

Thank you for the example of taking a break, Lord. Thank you for creating a day of rest and for urging us to take advantage of it.

In the name of Christ, amen.

About Max Lucado

More than 120 million readers have found inspiration and encouragement in the writings of Max Lucado. He lives with his wife, Denalyn, and their mischievous mutt, Andy, in San Antonio, Texas, where he serves the people of Oak Hills Church. Visit his website at MaxLucado.com or follow him at Twitter.com/MaxLucado and Facebook.com/MaxLucado.

About Jennifer K. Hale

Jennifer K. Hale is a Jesus-loving mama of three boys, happily married to her SuperHusband, Brian, for nearly fifteen years. As a passionate high school History and Social Studies teacher for many years, she's experienced the gamut of teaching highs and lows. Grateful to have been called by God into teaching and writing, she survives on chocolate and good books. You can get to know Jennifer at her blog, www.haleandheartywords.com.

Discover Even More Power in a Simple Prayer

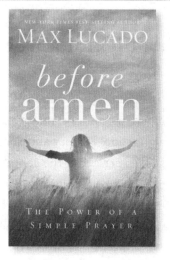

ISBN 978-0-7180-7812-6
$15.99

Join Max Lucado on a journey to the very heart of biblical prayer and discover rest in the midst of chaos and confidence even for prayer wimps.

Available wherever books are sold.

BeforeAmen.com

Make Your Prayers Personal

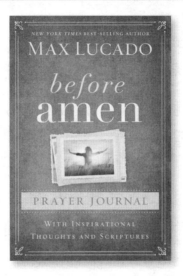

ISBN 978-0-7180-1406-3

$13.99

This beautiful companion journal to *Before Amen* helps readers stoke their prayer life. It features quotes and scriptures to inspire both prayer warriors and those who struggle to pray.

Tools for Your Church and Small Group

Before Amen: A DVD Study

ISBN 978-0-529-12342-8

$21.99

Max Lucado leads this four-session study through his discovery of a simple tool for connecting with God each day. This study will help small-group participants build their prayer life, calm the chaos of their world, and grow in Christ.

Before Amen Study Guide

ISBN 978-0-529-12334-3

$9.99

This guide is filled with Scripture study, discussion questions, and practical ideas designed to help small-group members understand Jesus' teaching on prayer. An integral part of the *Before Amen* small-group study, it will help group members build prayer into their everyday lives.

Before Amen
Church Campaign Kit

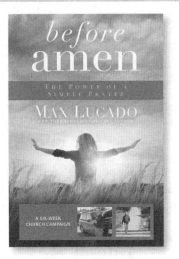

ISBN 978-0-529-12369-5

$49.99

The church campaign kit includes a four-session DVD study by Max Lucado; a study guide with discussion questions and video notes; the *Before Amen* trade book; a getting started guide; and access to a website with all the sermon resources churches need to launch and sustain a four-week *Before Amen* campaign.

Before Amen for Everyone

Before Amen Audiobook

ISBN 978-1-4915-4662-8 | $19.99

Enjoy the unabridged audio CD of *Before Amen*.

Before Amen eBook

ISBN 978-0-529-12390-9

Read *Before Amen* anywhere on your favorite tablet or electronic device.

Antes del amén Spanish Edition

ISBN 978-0-7180-0157-5 | $13.99

The hope of *Before Amen* is also available for Spanish-language readers.